NOW THAT YOU'VE GONE AND COME BACK

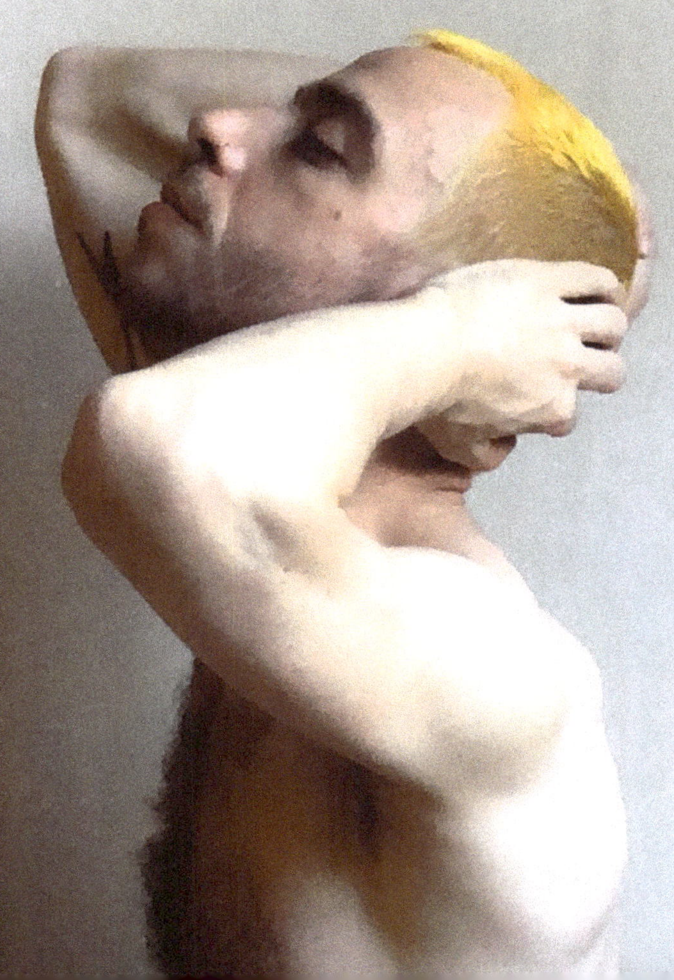

JONATHAN DAVID SMYTH

NOW THAT YOU'VE GONE AND COME BACK

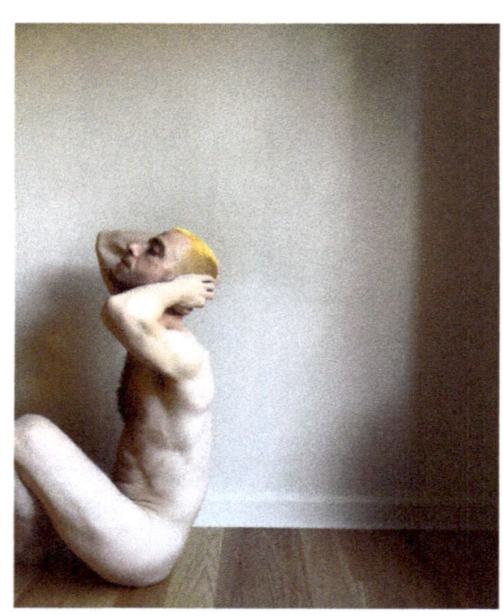

For my paternal grandmother, Jean
Smyth (née Strain), who liked to take
me for a wee paddle in the Irish Sea.

"I thought the most beautiful thing
in the world must be shadow, the
million moving shapes and cul-de-sacs
of shadow. There was shadow in bureau
drawers and closets and suitcases,
and shadow under houses and trees
and stones, and shadow at the back of
people's eyes and smiles, and shadow,
miles and miles and miles of it, on
the night side of the earth."

—Sylvia Plath
The Bell Jar

"Between my finger and my thumb
The squat pen rests.
I'll dig with it."

—Seamus Heaney
Digging from Death of a Naturalist

STATEMENT

This book comprises two primary projects: a
photographic series titled *Between You and Me*, and
an ongoing collection of works on paper called
One-to-One.

Between You and Me (2019–2020) is a series
of nude self-portraits inspired by finding and
reconnecting with my birth mother. Each portrait
is an expression of myself and of a certain key
figure from my life. In addition to my birth mother,
these include my late adoptive father, a fiercely
independent man despite being born with part of his
left arm missing; my foster sisters, who survived
years of domestic abuse and trauma, and who were
my biggest champions growing up; and my biological
father, whom I have never met but am nonetheless
intrinsically connected to.

Before re-meeting my biological mom at the age
of 30, I'd never encountered a direct physical
resemblance between me and another person.
Afterwards, I found it nearly impossible to not

see her face when I looked at myself in the mirror. This led me to think about the idea of family in its many configurations, how other people can mentor us or deter us, and how shared circumstances and stories can affect and shape us as individuals. While considering my own past experiences, I also felt the need to create a project that simply documented how I feel inside today: more strong, present, and open than ever before.

One-to-One (2016—present) is a series of handwritten pieces, begun in earnest when I was a child. Back then I had a habit of jotting down words that I liked the look of, and it has now become a lifelong habit.

I was ten years old when my foster sisters, Tanya and Kathy, left home abruptly and in quick succession. Their absence caused me to turn inwards, and I felt somehow responsible for their leaving, too. It would be years before I had contact with them again, and in the interim, I found myself going through items that they had left behind: cassette tapes, photographs, and a hefty collection of young adult books. What began as a coping mechanism became a sort of obsession with record-keeping: I would study my sisters' books at length, copying certain words and phrases into my notepad. As I got older, I started to record bits and pieces from real-life conversations, too. I wrote down unfamiliar words and sayings, quizzing people about what they meant or where they came

from. I spent one summer holiday carrying around a
thesaurus, reading it cover-to-cover as though it
were a novel.

By the time I was an undergraduate in the late
2000s, collecting language in this way had become
second nature to me. Using my mobile phone like a
diary, I began texting myself sentences or single
words that I wanted to remember. I also started to
notice the relationships between photographs and
text, pulling words from signage or advertisements
that I could later reuse. In a way, I was creating
a mood board with text: many of my projects' titles
have originated from this linguistic archive,
which I now keep as a digital, searchable document.

I never stopped using a pen and paper, though. This
is the format presented in *One-to-One*—a partial
survey of my archive of collected words and
phrases from the past six years. Each piece has
been photographed for inclusion in this book.

Jonathan David Smyth
West Hollywood, CA
31 August 2022

WHEN I LOOK DOWN AT MY HANDS I CAN SEE YOU.

My first memory is of being in hospital as a baby. I read once that children who have experienced traumatic events can retain early memories because they weren't able to physically speak about it at the time. Do you have any memories like that?

It is Christmas 1989—my second year of life. I shimmy out of my enormous hospital bed to follow the sound of what I think is your voice. I hear it reverberate from the end of a long, dimly lit corridor that is outstretched in front of me. I don't know how to walk or talk, but I am determined to keep going. Everything reeks of antiseptic; I can almost taste it in my mouth. I am wearing an oversized, floral blue gown. The thin cottony material trails behind my little body as I crawl on hands and knees. The linoleum floor's stiff coldness makes me shiver, and my tiny hands stick with each primitive movement. On my right arm, there is a tight wristband with "Infant Scott" hastily written in black ballpoint ink.

You said you've always been a night owl. Did you have a hard time sleeping as a child? I did. I would lie awake for hours, pretending I was somewhere else. I'd sometimes sleepwalk around the house, too, or have awful dreams of getting lost or left alone. I still have nightmares like this sometimes.

Growing up, my sisters Tanya, Kathy, and Jenna shared a bedroom. Kathy and Jenna were in a red, rackety metal bunk bed, and Tanya, the oldest, had a single to herself. Next door, I had my own blue "boy" bedroom, kitted out with football wallpaper and matching memorabilia that never interested me. I could hear my sisters whispering and sniggering through the walls. I would go to their bedroom door with my best friend Foxy in hand, begging them to let me in. Eventually they opened the door, and I'd squeeze in beside Tanya and quickly go to sleep. Sometimes, we would wake our adoptive father, John, who'd then swiftly escort me back to my room. As I lay down in bed, I'd hear my sisters through the wall again, saying how sorry they felt for me, and that I shouldn't be alone. It always made me cry.

I, too, had a bunk bed. Looking up at the empty top
mattress above, I would begin to visualize some
other place for me to go that didn't feel so empty,
somewhere full of color. I'd play a game with the
orange, fluorescent lights from the streetlamps,
which sliced the mattress into thick pieces,
leaving some lit up and some in shadow. My stuffed
toys were my playmates, and I'd talk to them until
I fell asleep.

I would think of you most at night, wondering where
you were and feeling a strong but inarticulable
connection between us. On nights that I
sleepwalked, I'd wake up suddenly and realize that
I was in a completely different part of the house.
Alison, my adoptive mother, once woke up to me
standing in her bedroom at 3:00 am, carrying my
pillow like a suitcase and announcing that I was
going away on holiday. I must have been about six.

**I never once considered that I might not see you
again. To me, every excursion was an opportunity
to bump into you. Do you think you would have
recognized me?**

At the shopping center, I'd wander away from my
parents and sisters. I would stroll the premises
by myself, "collecting" other families I liked
the look of. I would pick out different dream-mums,
ranking them in a list as the day went on.

Having a second set of parents you've never met
comes with a certain kind of excitement. The
idea of running into them one day keeps you on
constant lookout. For me, the possibility of such
an encounter didn't feel so remote. Occasionally,
I'd follow strangers to try and glimpse some germ
of myself in them, something physical that I could
relate to. I'd get utterly lost in this easter-egg
hunt for you, which remained a hobby of mine for
many years. I felt guilty when my adoptive parents
caught me staring, thinking they knew exactly what
I was plotting.

**I began to write poetry and lyrics around the age
of 10. I always enjoyed writing and it came to me
easily, but for years was too afraid to show it
to anyone but a handful of friends. Did you keep
a diary or a journal? I kept notepads with me all
the time, jotting down rhymes and phrases I liked
the sound of. I still do this today in my artwork.**

I was four years old when I learned to spell my
first word. The word came to me in thick black
letters on pink cardstock paper, neatly enclosed
by my teacher inside a small, brown paper envelope.
This was my first homework assignment. The
directions were simple: Learn how to spell your
assigned word and say it aloud in class.

"L-O-O-K," I said to Alison one night, practicing for the occasion. It was Friday—bath night. "L-O-O-K. Look." I said it back once more. "But what does it mean?" I asked. Alison turned away from me and glanced over at John, who was half-watching a game show on T.V.

"It means to see something or someone," Tanya cut in matter-of-factly. She was sitting cross-legged on the floor of the living room, reading a novel by the fire.

"I'm *looking* at you," Kathy, my other sister, weighed in. "And you're *looking* at me." Kathy was on the other side of the room, brushing the knots out of Jenna's wet hair.

"Jonathan, look at me. I can see you," Tanya said, sitting up now and looking directly at me. Alison nodded in agreement, seeming grateful for the help. I recited the word again: "L-O-O-K. *Look*."

"That's-a-boy!" John said proudly, giving me a thumbs up, because I really did understand.

On the day we met in person for the first time, I woke up with a small rash on my stomach—an anxious reaction I'd get as a child. You said that you were nervous, too, but to me, you seemed so cool and collected. I remember thinking how surreal it was: meeting my mother for the first time at thirty-one. After learning that you'd never had a chance to know your own mother, I felt even more grateful.

I'll never forget the first time I saw your face. I was about twelve years old, riffling through storage boxes, when I found an unused leather-clad book. When I opened it, two color photographs fell out and landed at my feet. I instinctively picked one of them up; it was a snapshot of a young woman sitting on a large pillar by the seaside. This woman looked thoughtful and striking, and as I studied her, an immediate feeling of recognition came over me. It was a feeling that I had not experienced before. It was like looking at a photograph of myself that I had no memory of taking.

I didn't tell anyone about the photo, but I
returned to it many times during my teenage years.
I haven't seen it in a long time, but I don't need
to; it is forever etched in my brain. Even though
you and I have many physical differences, your face
has become part of me. I think this is what people
mean when they talk about a mother-child bond.
You gave me life but didn't raise me. We share
a history but no core memories. I was afraid we
would have nothing in common, but when I look down
at my hands, I can see you.

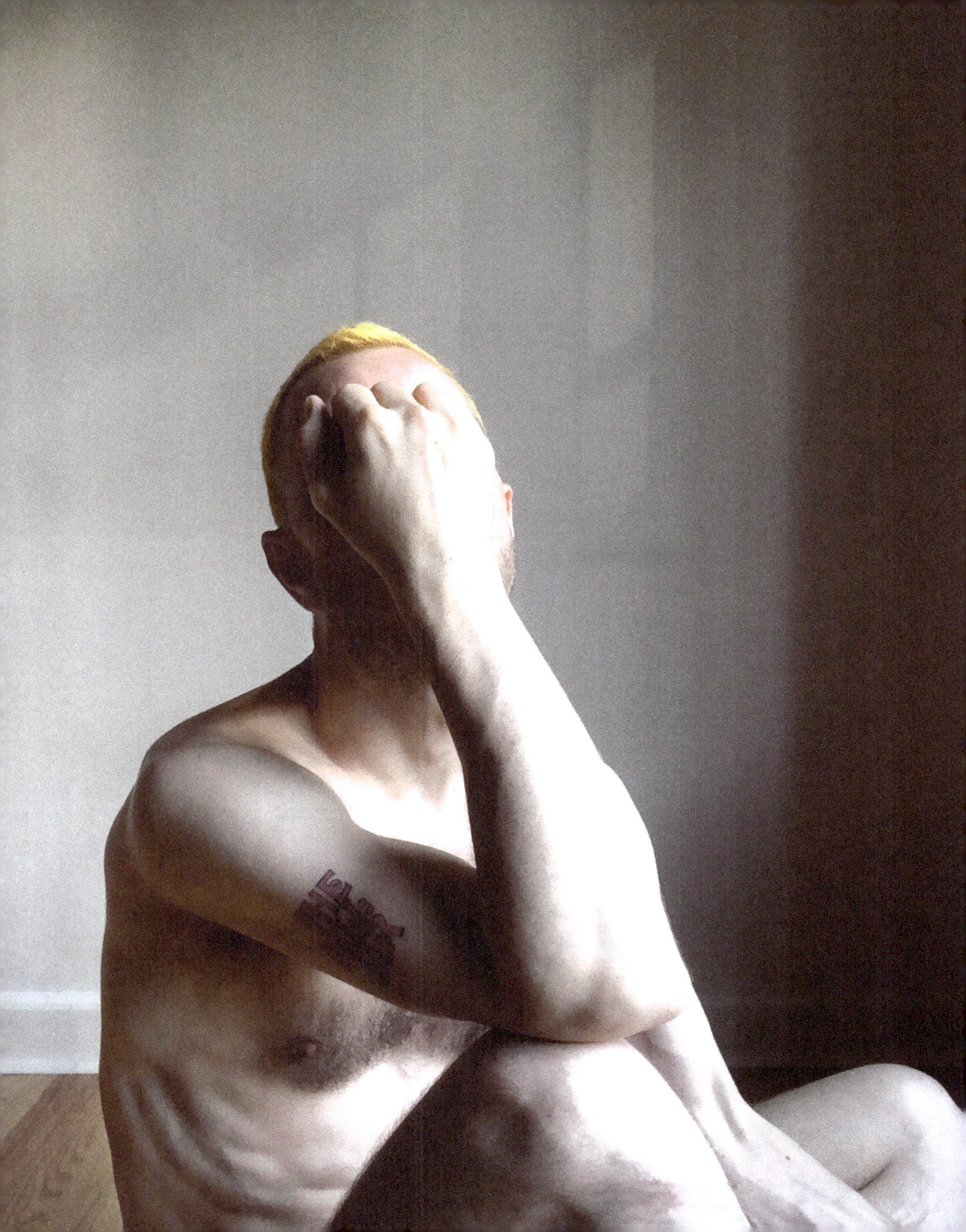

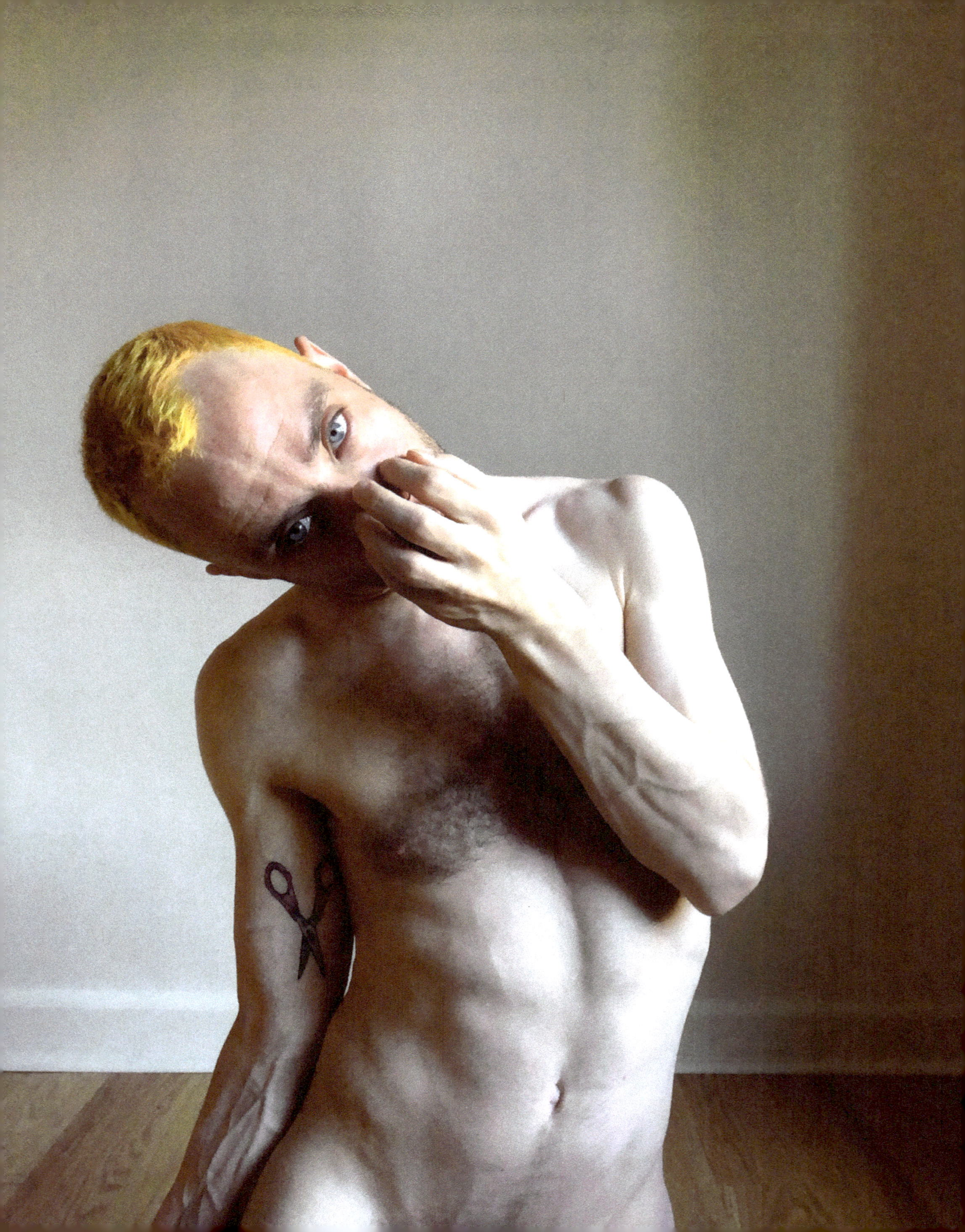

Sticking
out.

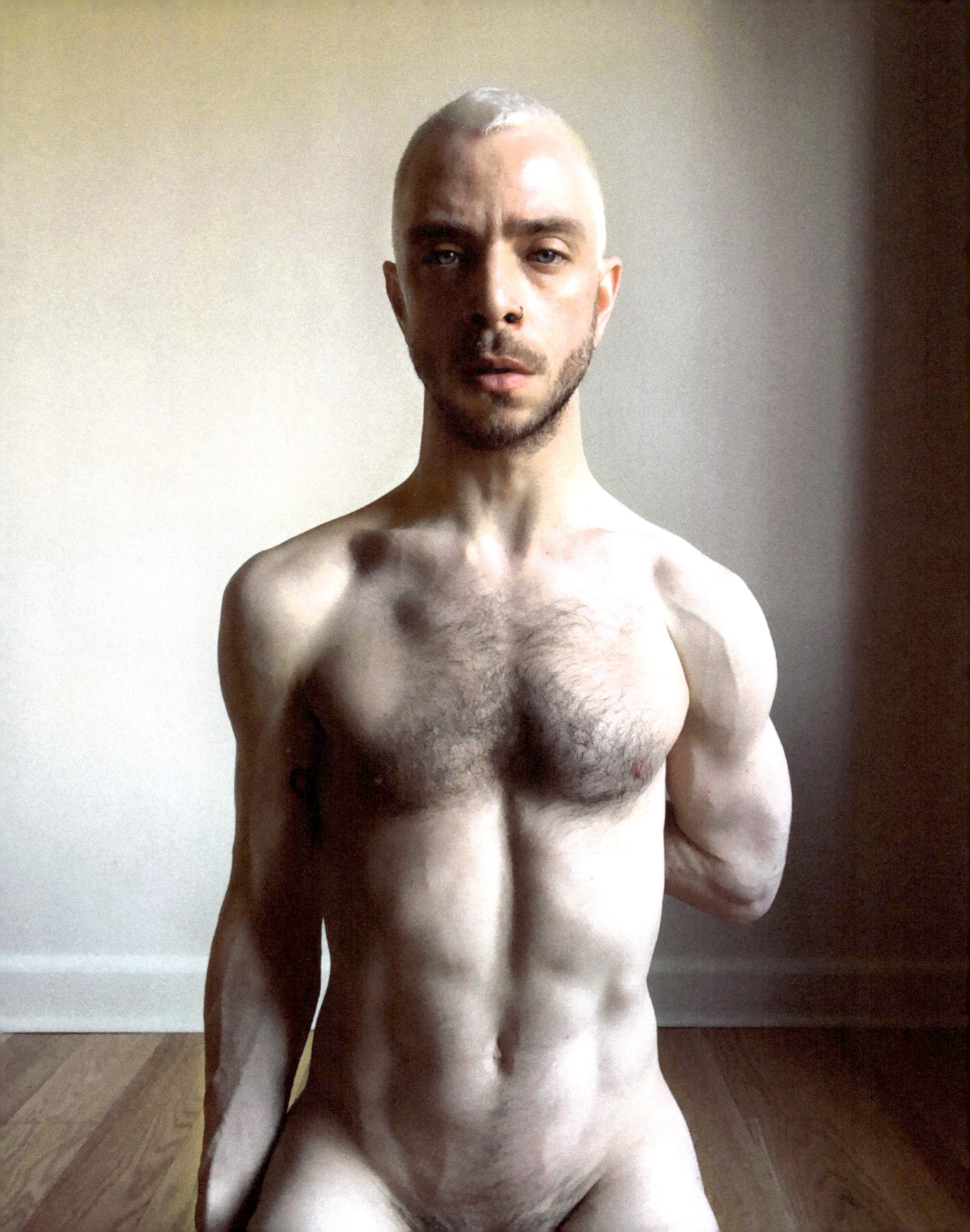

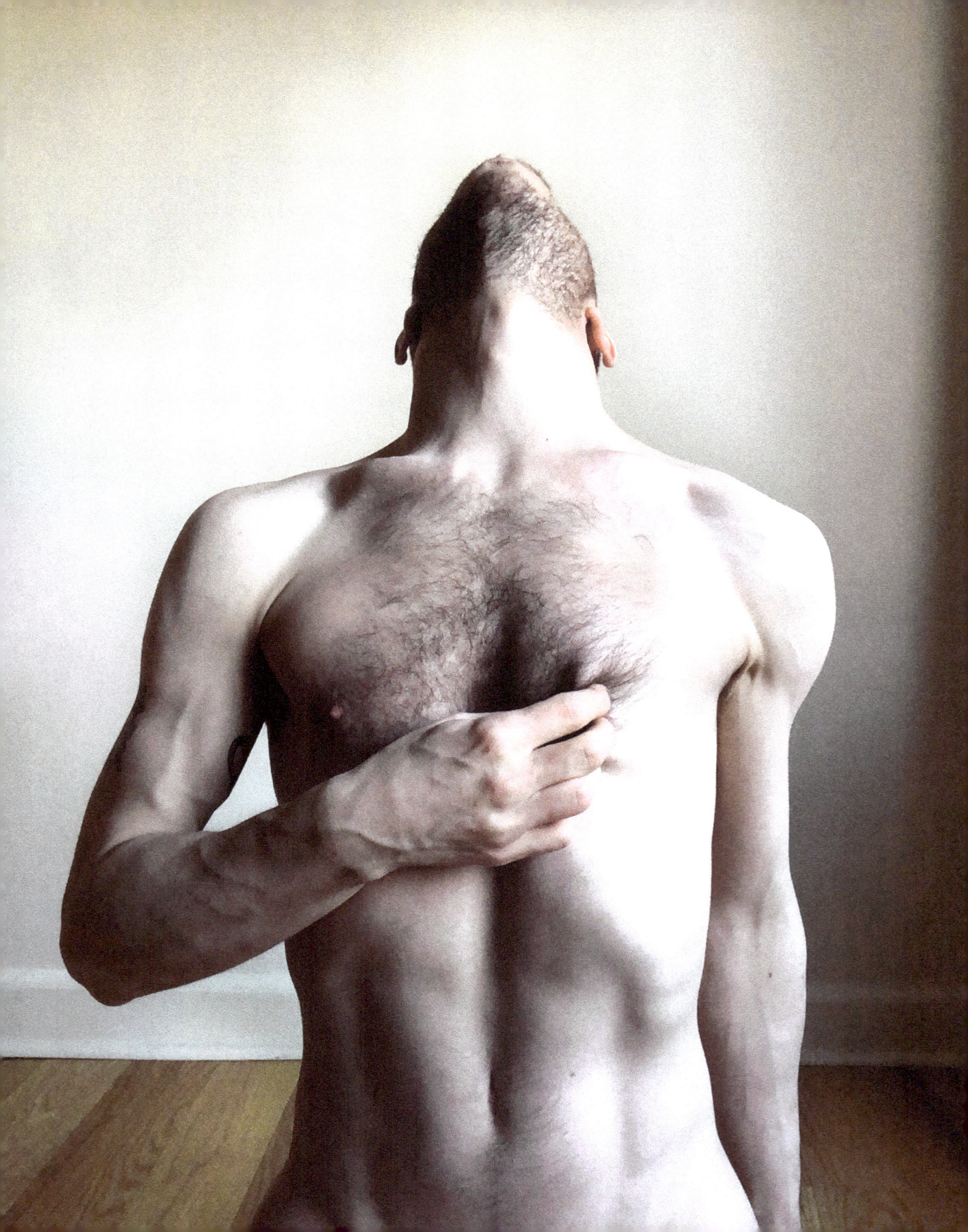

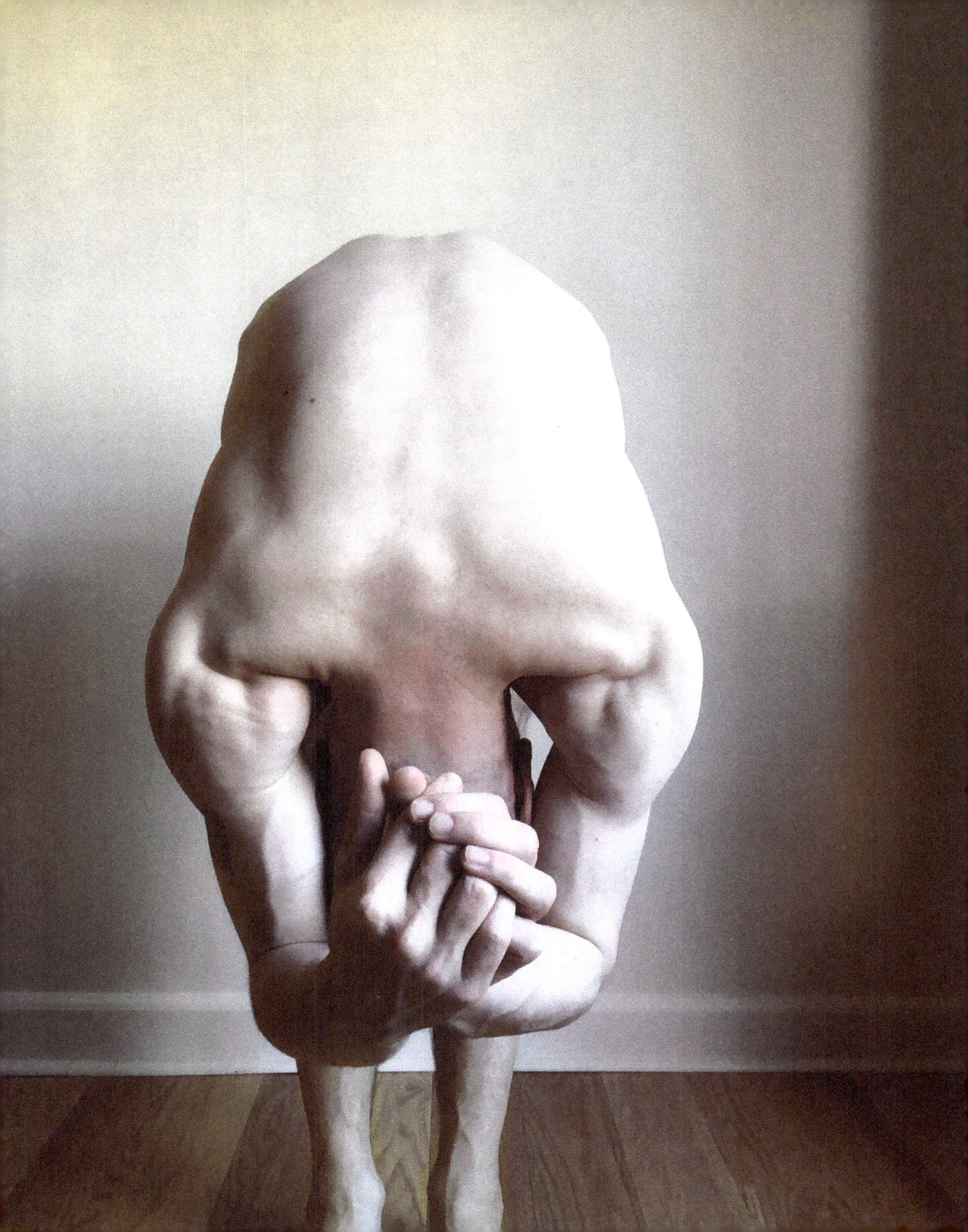

Left,
Right,
And Centre.

There's
A want
About you.

Hard on
you

Hard on
me.

ALMOST HOME

My glasses are fogged up something shocking,
And the dense, dewy grass
Attaches itself to my black leather boots.

They marry, and dance,
    And carry on.

Traipsing through muck,
Avoiding potholes and path water,
I remind myself that I've hand-picked
This route along the waterside.

                And it makes me giggle.

I've been told time and again
To steer clear of this place...

This dangerous dwelling,

        but how can I stay away from
        this dander of delights?

Still, it would be hard for anyone to ignore the
Dully drills of engines and sirens nearby.

They have rallied together.
        Half-hidden faces.

I can count them on one hand.

And as I begin to approach the stony steps
That start where the river ends,

I feel like I'm almost at home

        In this newfangled, noisy place.

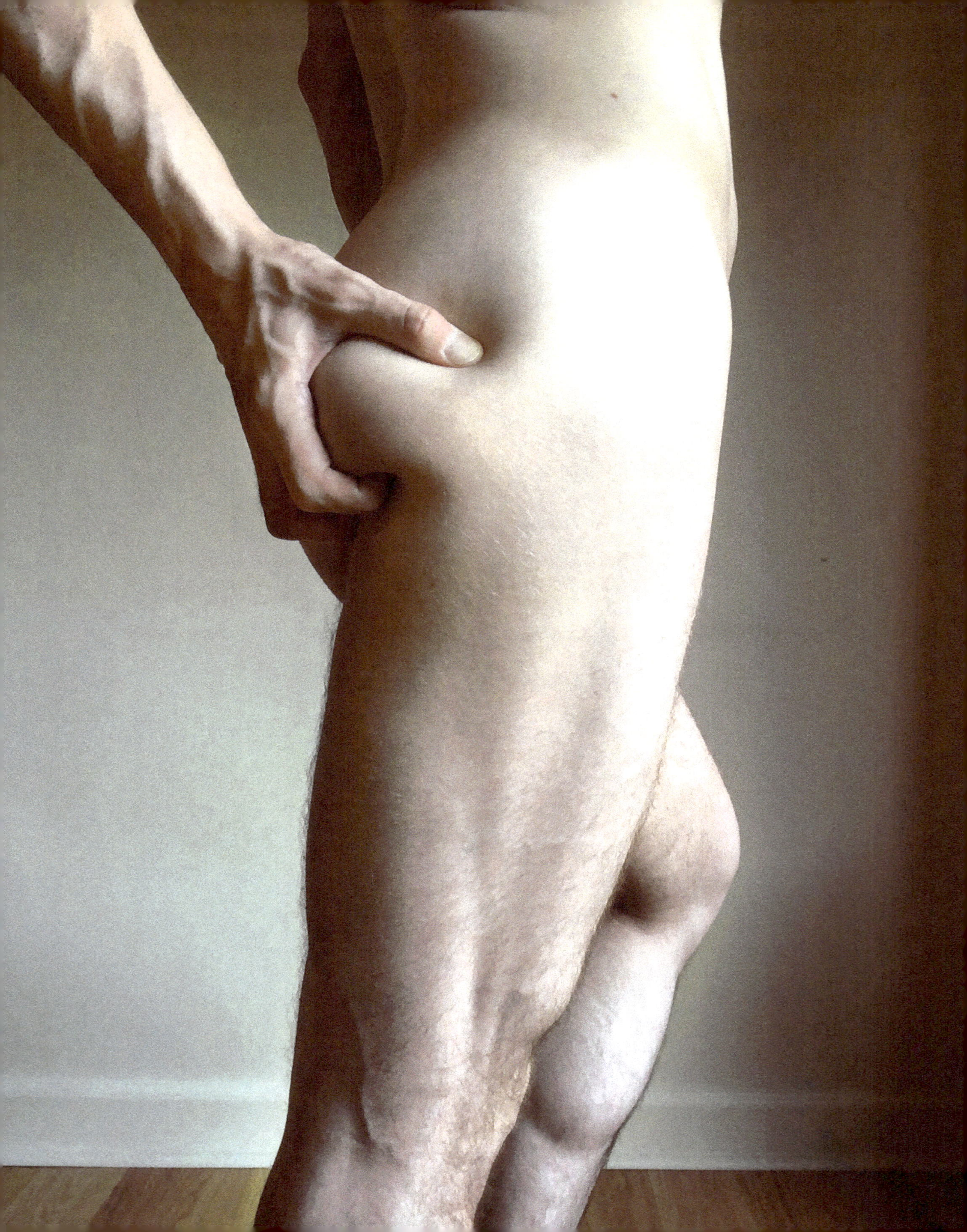

I love you
so much

—JA.

on the
outs.

All
The
Rage.

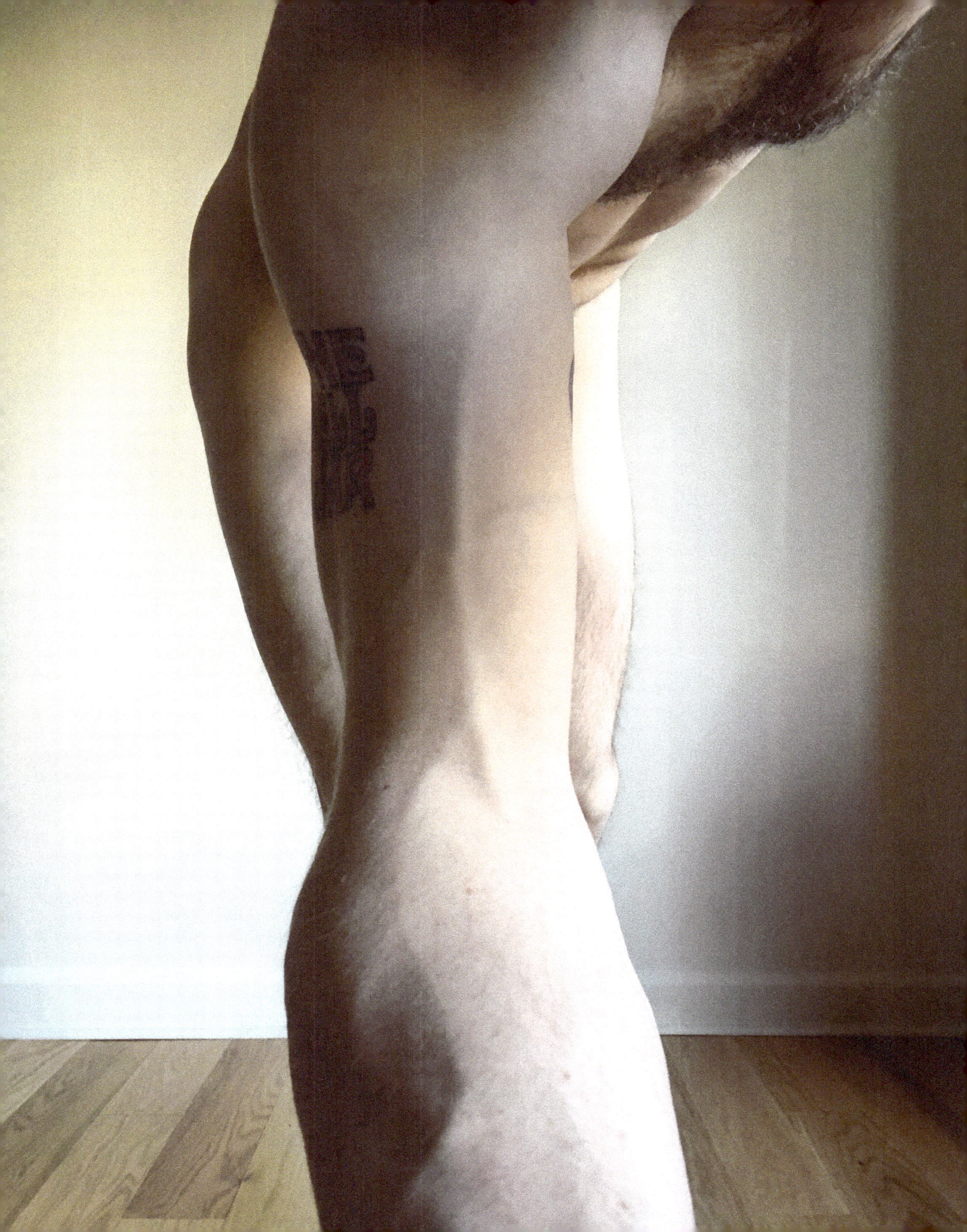

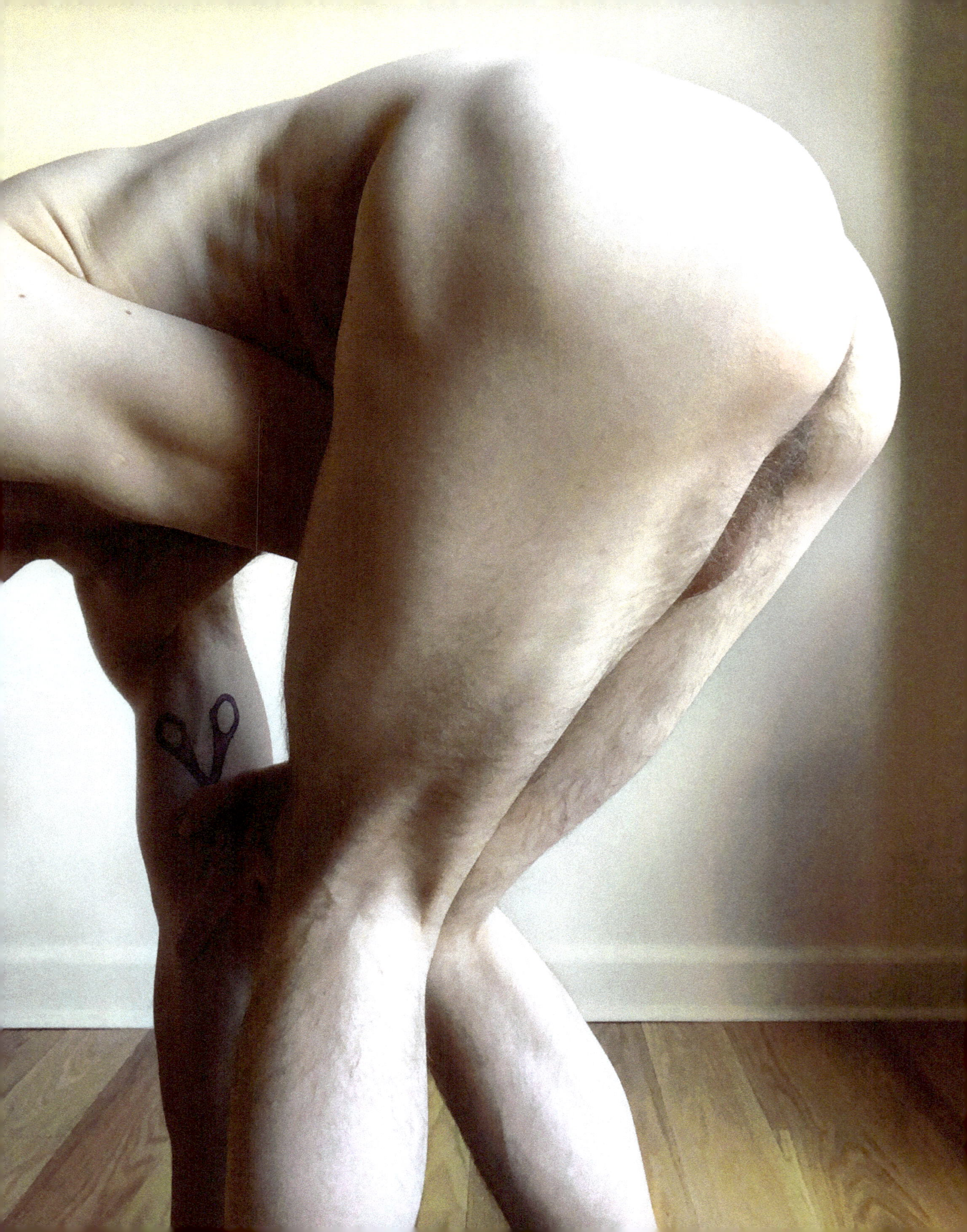

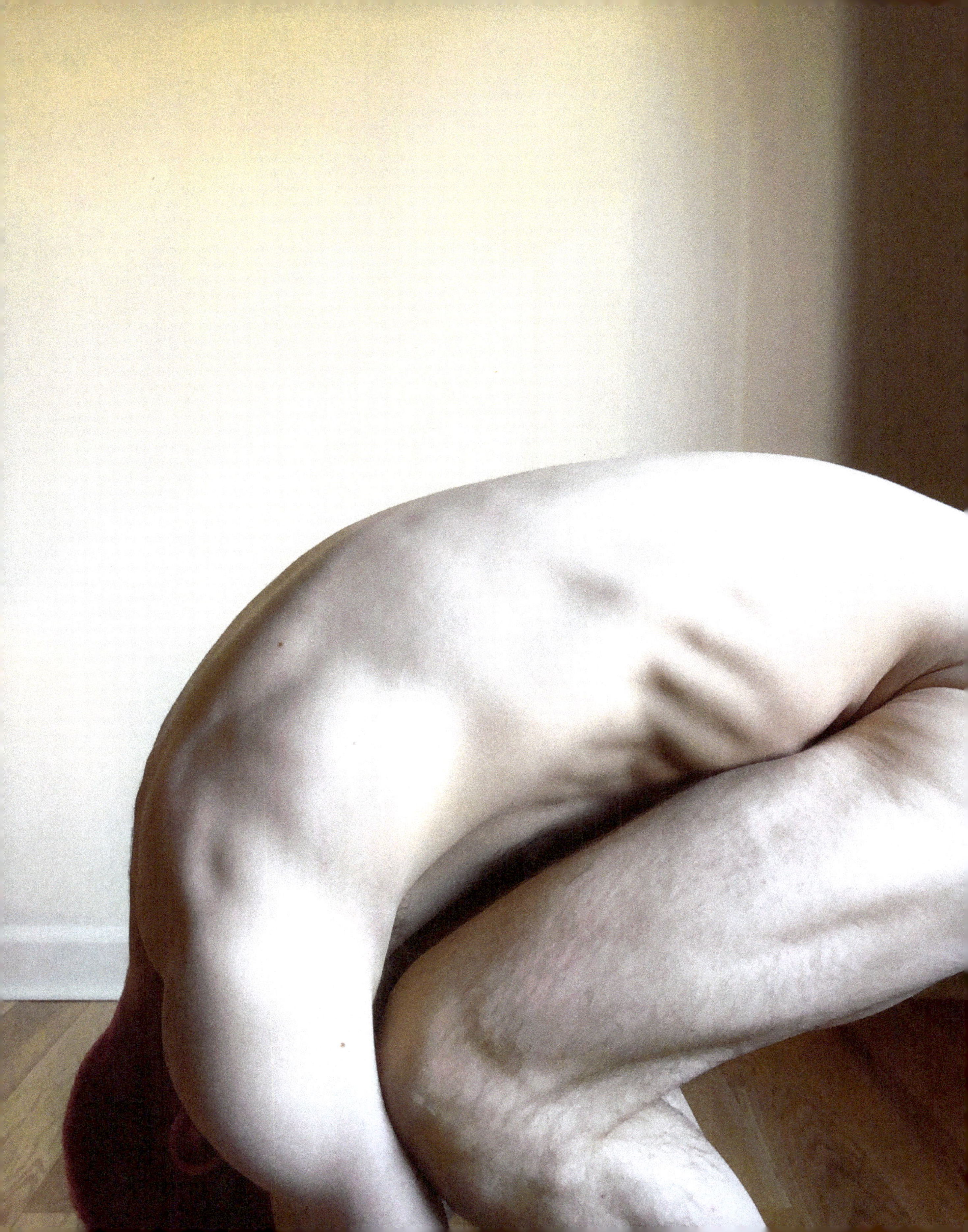

Ghosting.

Ghosting.

Ghosting.

Make
Amends.

Make
Amends.

Make Amends.
Make Amends.

WOKE ME UP A LITTLE

Things had blurred a little
Felt a tiny bit lost
Was a bit unsettled
In what I wanted most

But you pulled a tight focus
Shined a light in my eyes
I was feeling hopeless
Now I'm putting up a fight

You woke me up a little
Your words were like a trigger
I'm feeling so much better
And now I will remember

It's easy to become distracted
From what you want to do
Life can hand you a million chances
And take them away from you

But you revitalized my vision
You helped me decide
It was done with such precision
I'm taking great big strides

You woke me up a little
Your words were like a trigger
I'm feeling so much better
And now I will remember

You woke me up a little
Had myself in such a pickle
You told me I could handle
You led by fine example

It can be discouragingly tragic
When heartache comes at you in waves
Slipping back into old habits
Not dealing with the pain

But you stood tall and persisted
You grabbed a hold of my hand
I was jaded and indifferent
Now I'm back in command

You woke me up a little
Your words were like a trigger
I'm feeling so much better
And now I will remember

You woke me up a little
Felt so caught in the middle
You watched me turn a corner
And now I'm that much stronger.

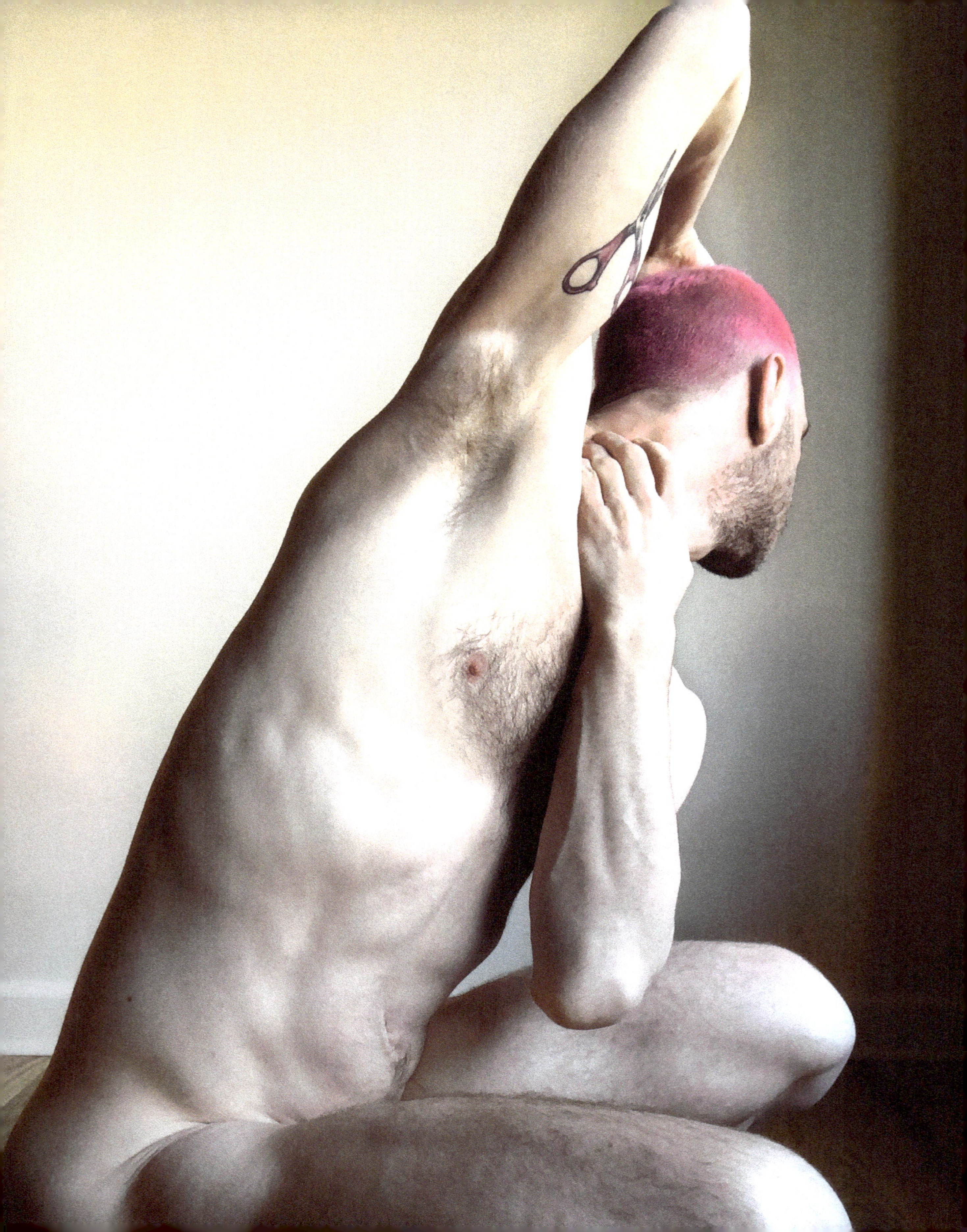

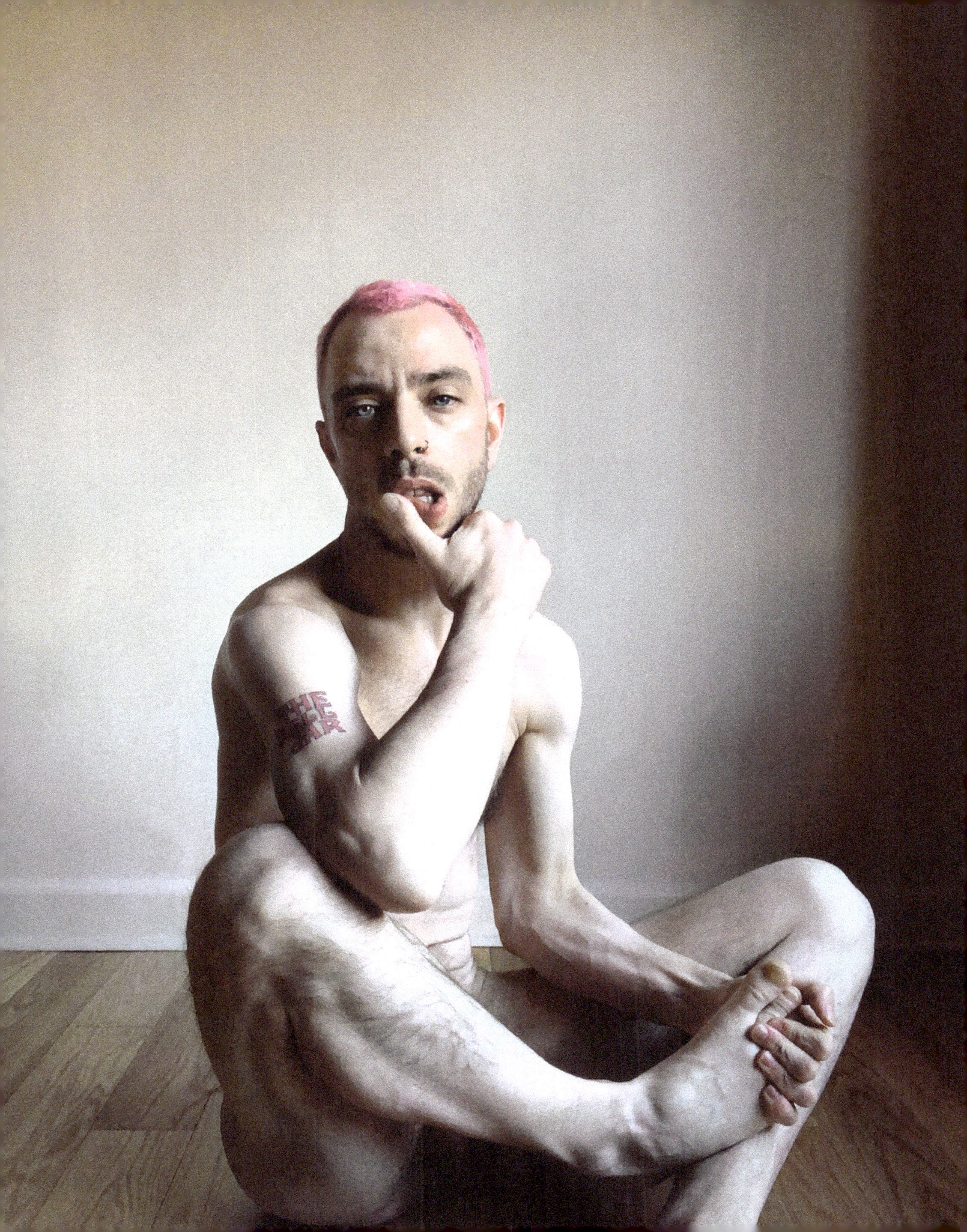

use
me
Re-use
me.

Needs
Must.

No one
Asked
you.

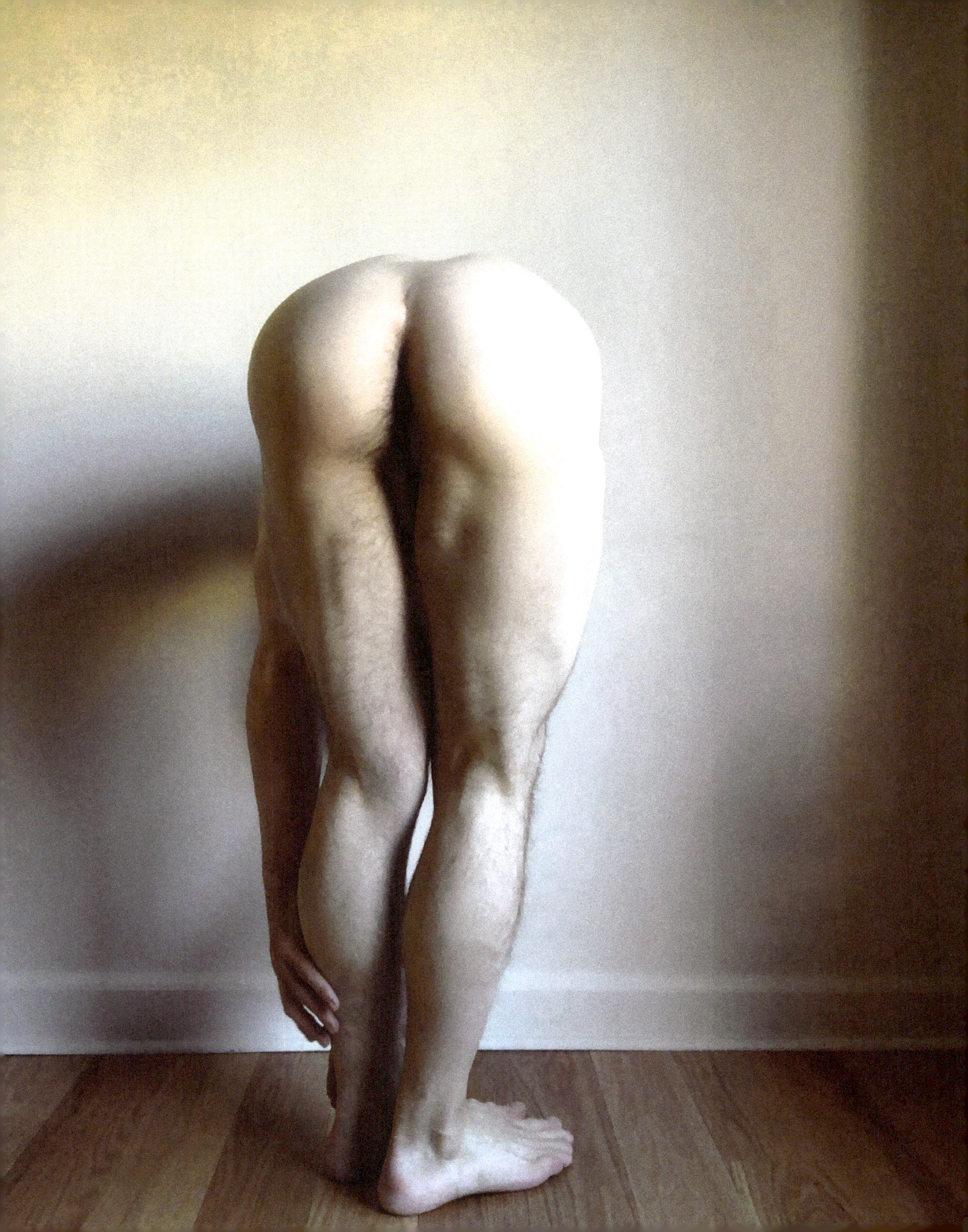

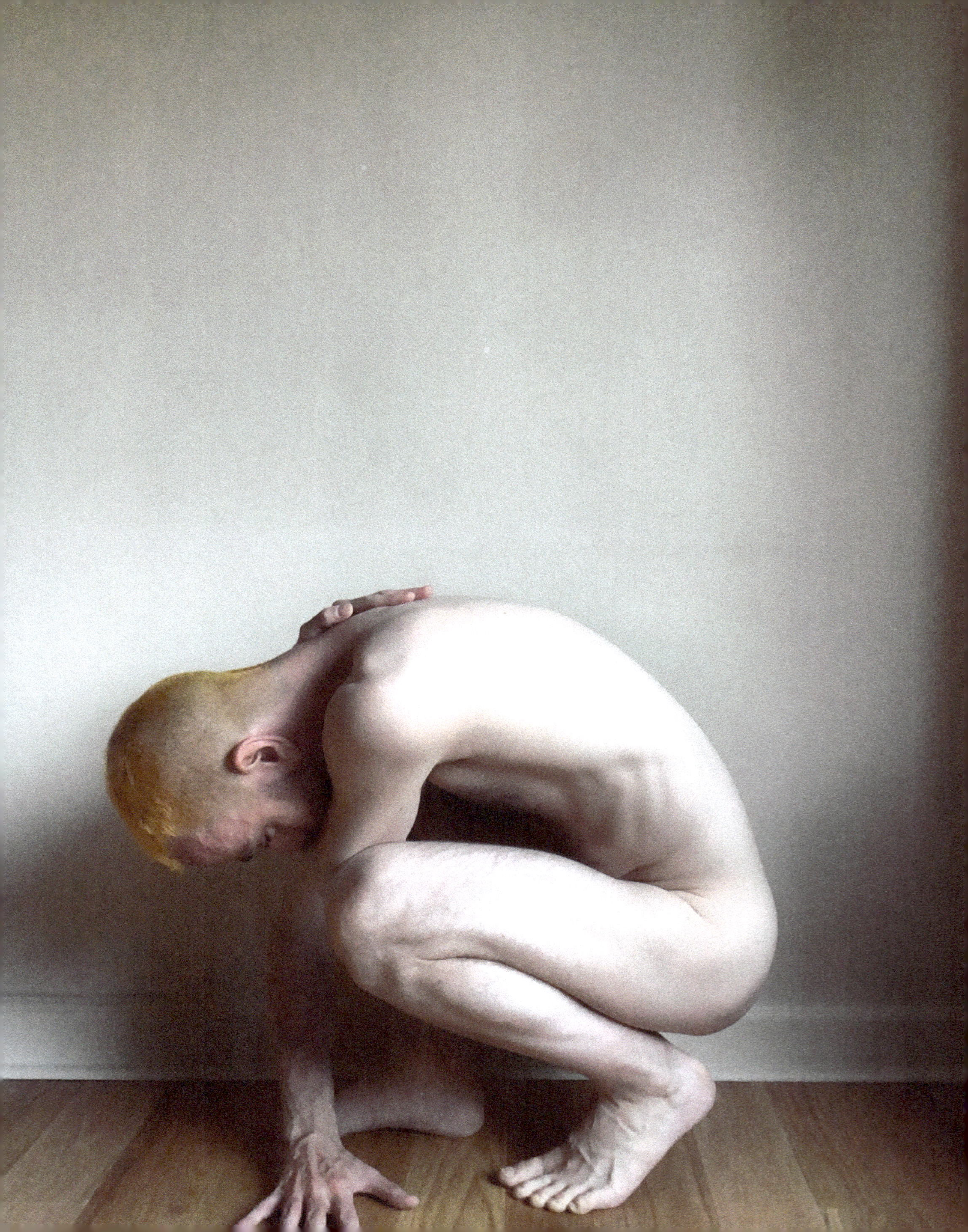

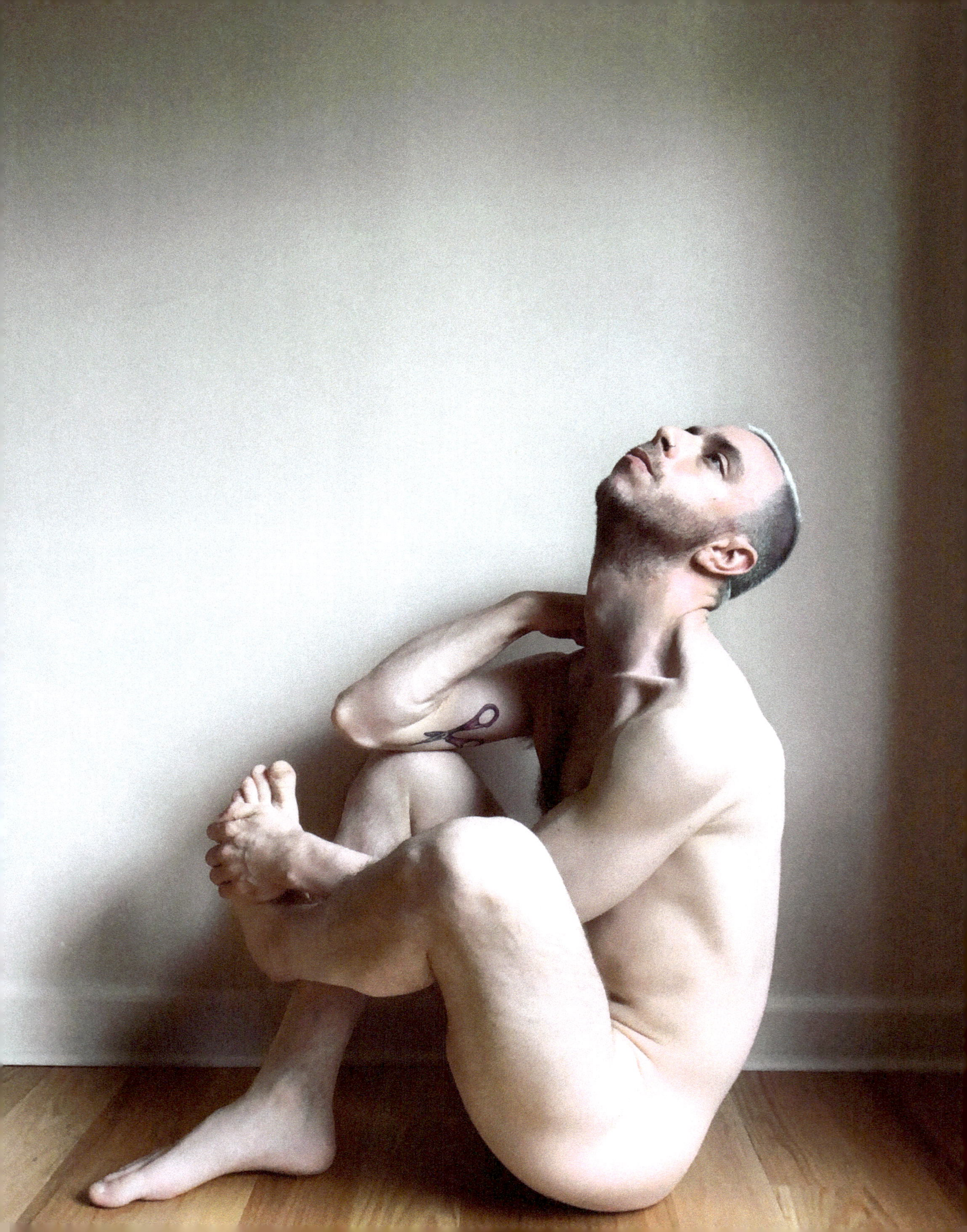

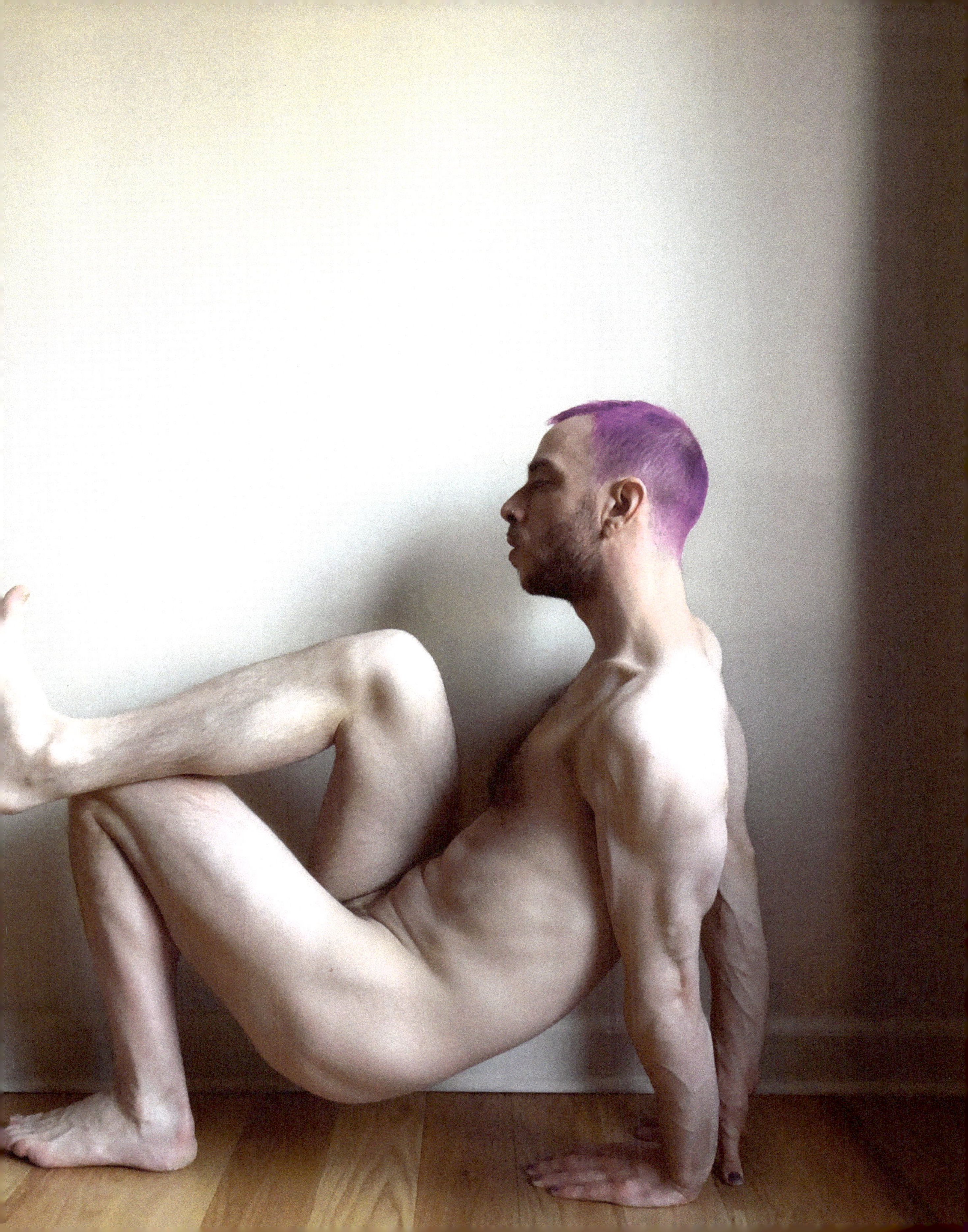

I feel
like i'm
losing you.

What a
Pair We'd
make.

IN TWO MINDS

The sight of you.
The fear of you.
The newness of you.
The reluctance of you.
The tenacity of you.
The failure of you.
The thrill of you.
The weight of you.
The rejection of you.

The surprise of you.

The sound of you.
The promise of you.
The absence of you.
The fantasy of you.
The demand of you.
The anticipation of you.
The ambivalence of you.
The warmth of you.
The danger of you.

The benefits of you.

The touch of you.
The curiosity of you.
The hindrance of you.
The strength of you.
The vulnerability of you.
The persistence of you.
The kindness of you.
The criticism of you.
The safeguarding of you.

The significance of you.

<u>The acceptance of you.</u>

Take it
on the
face.

Take
me
I'm
yours.

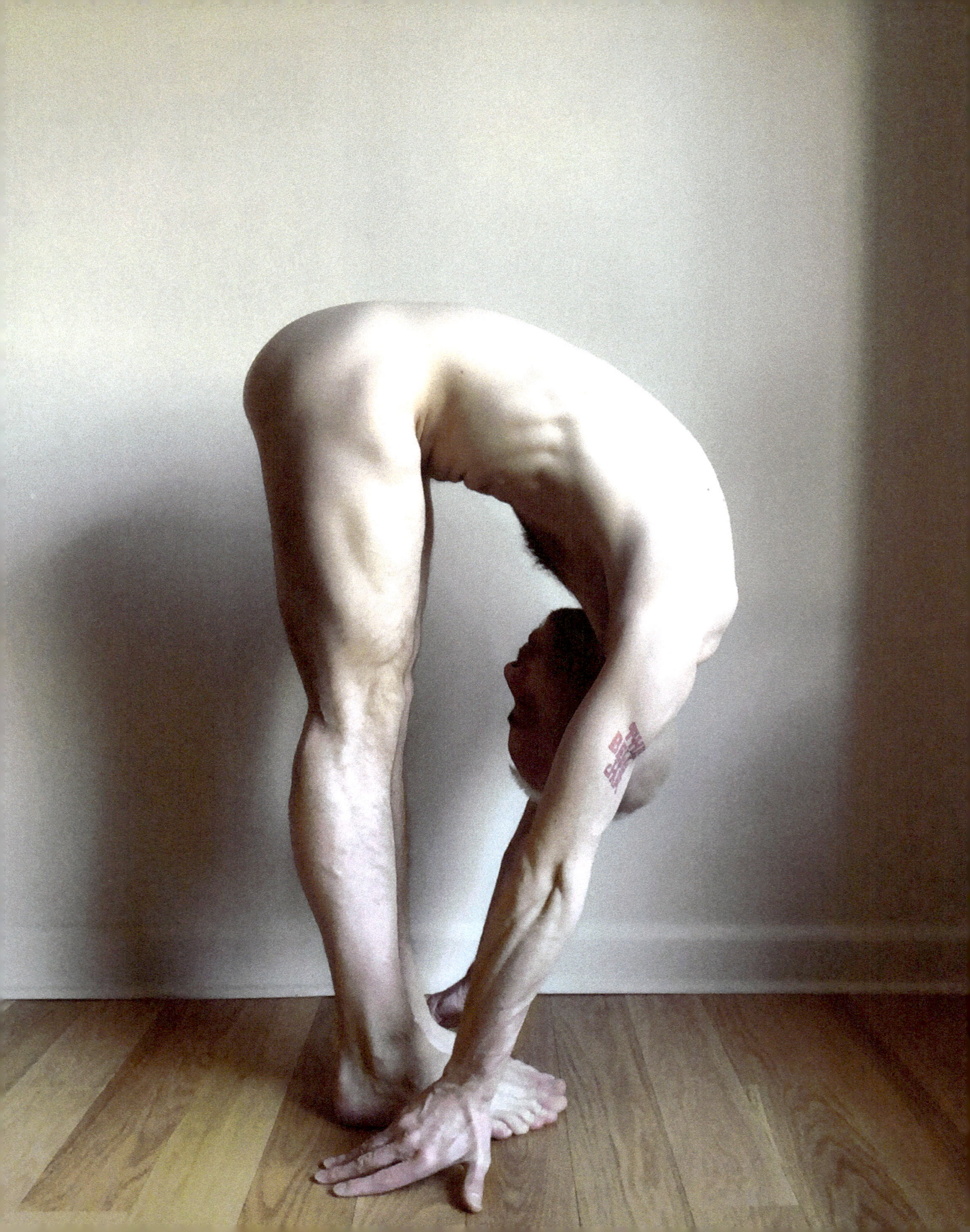

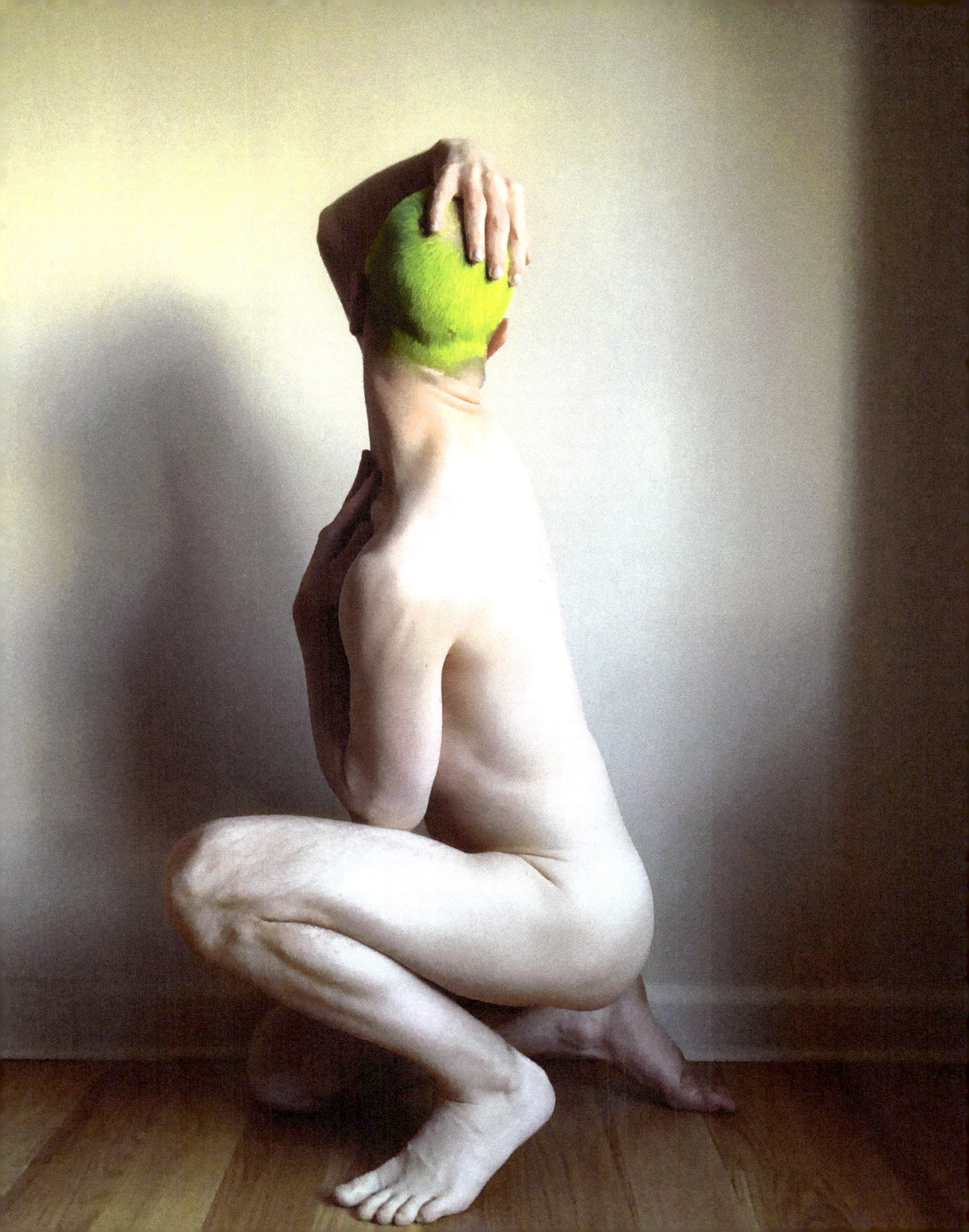

More
fool
you.

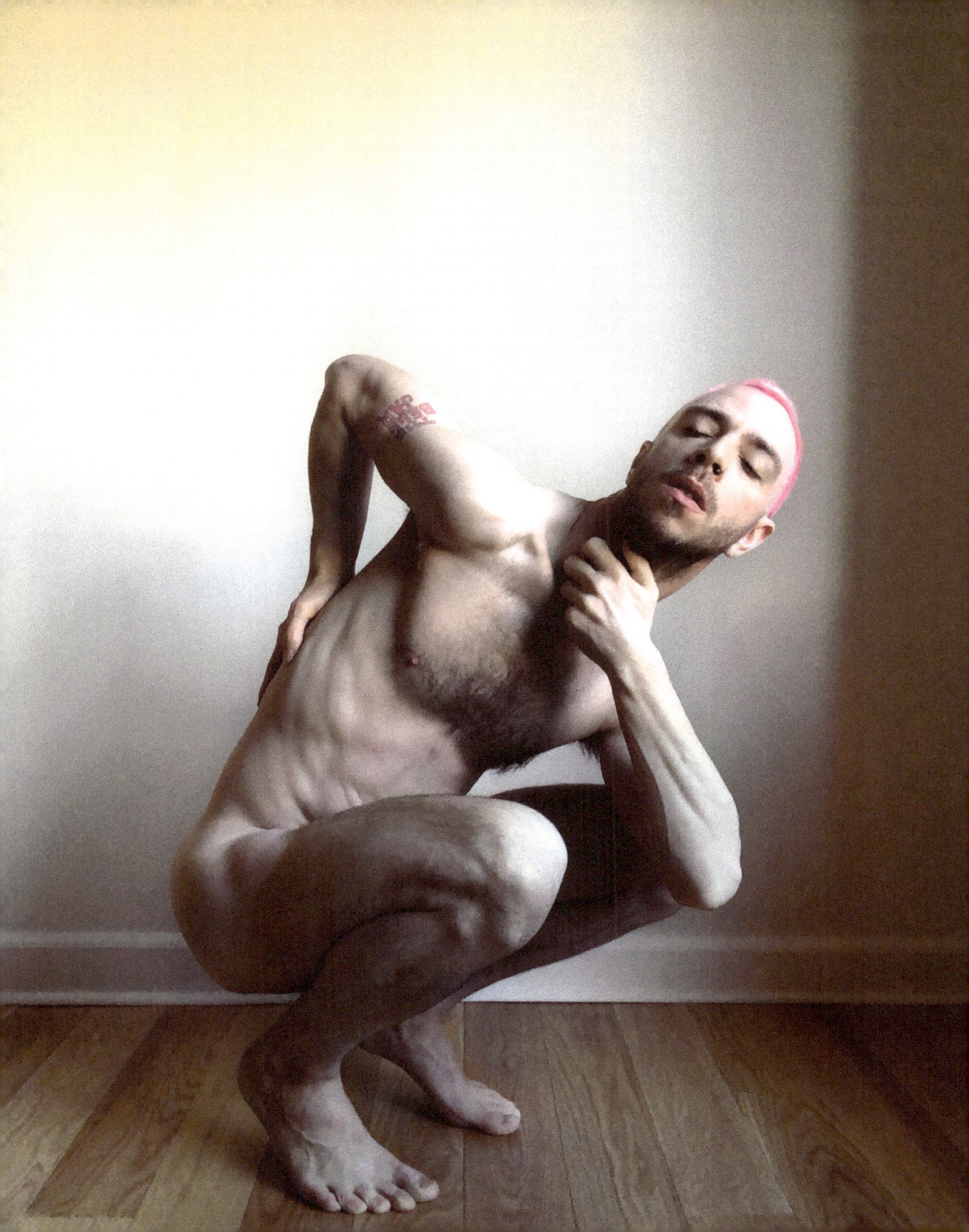

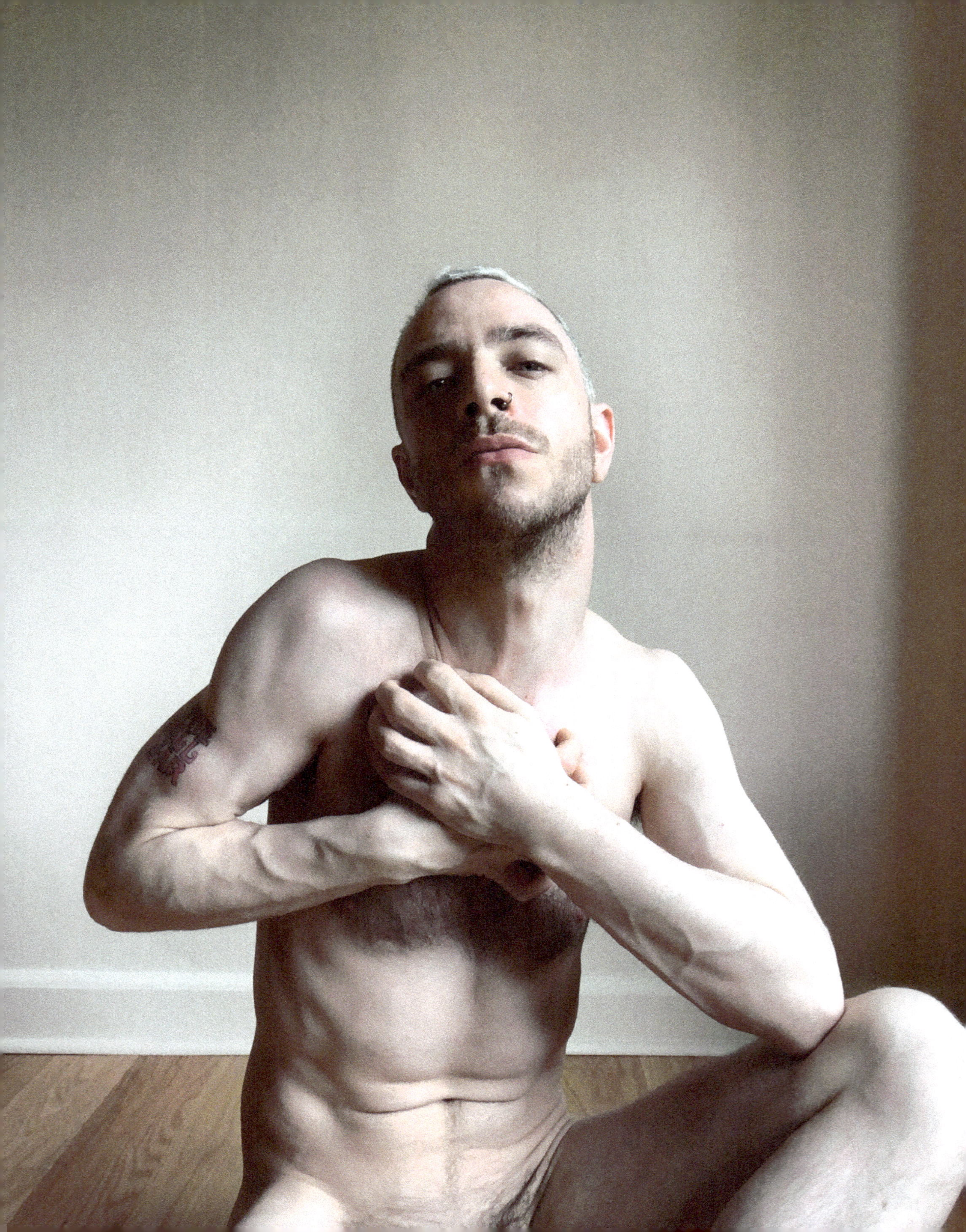

Not
going
Anywhere .

Not
popular
Enough.

Anchored
to you.

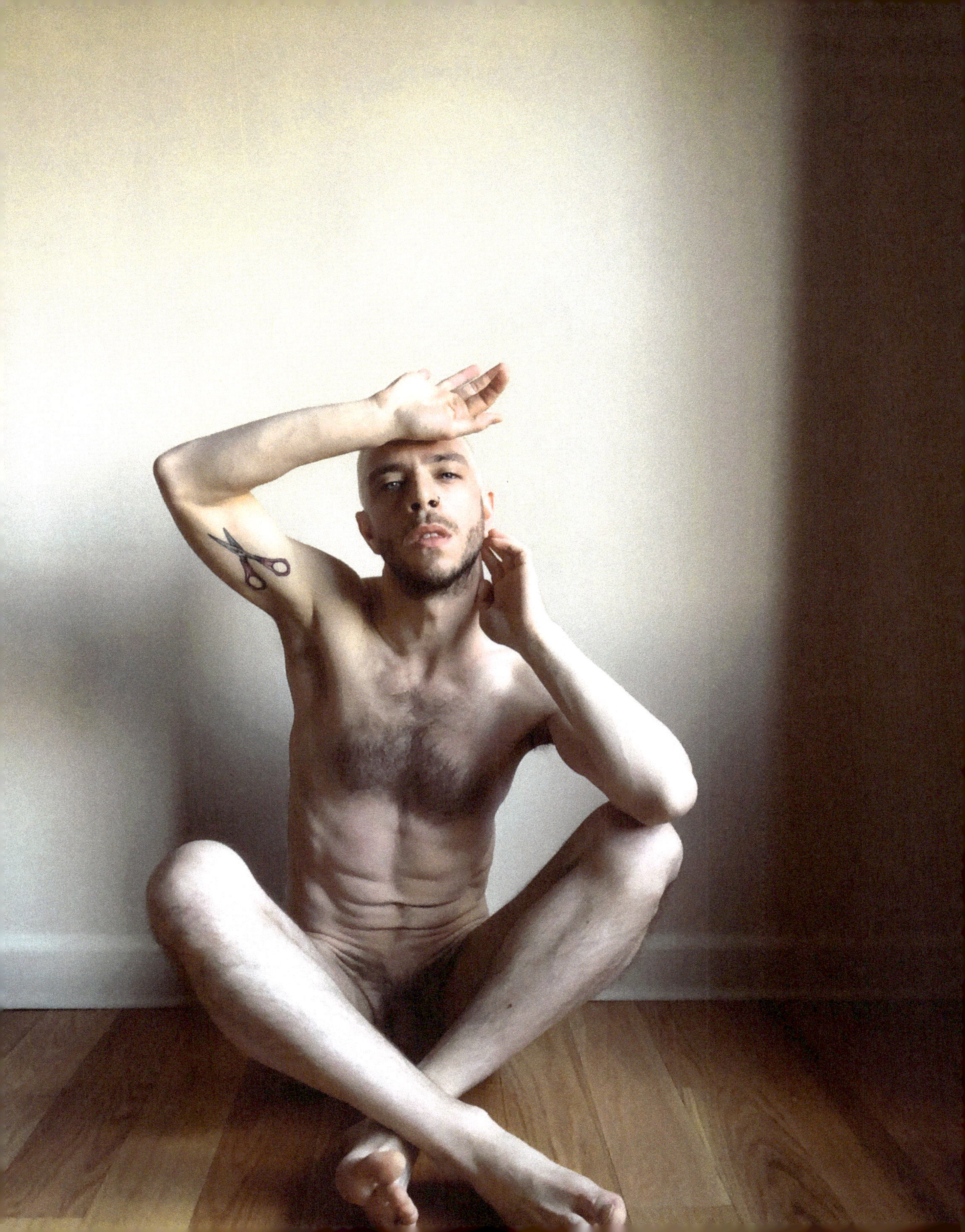

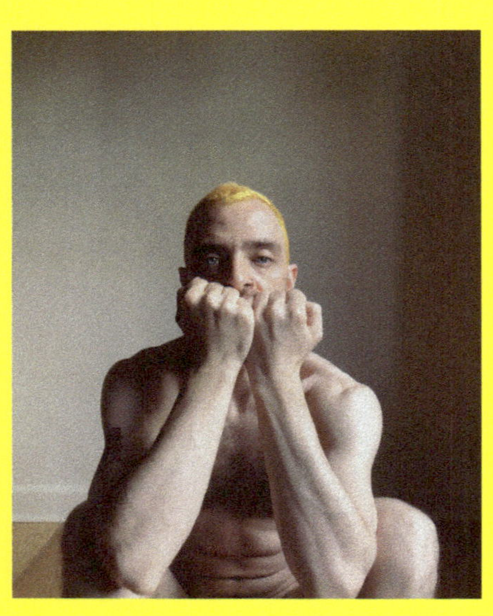

ACKNOWLEDGEMENTS

I'd like to thank the following people for their encouragement, love, and support throughout the making of this book:

Gio Black Peter, Perry Brass, Eric Brown, Tara Champion, Shari Diamond, Michelle Dunn Marsh, Steven Evans, Allen Frame, Corinne Furnari, Richard Haines, Hunter Lee Hughes, Stephanie Kaznocha, June Kim, Shelley Kinkead, Michael Moreno, Stiofan O'Ceallaigh, Jody Poorwill, Ernesto Pujol, Eric Rhein, Robert Ritter, Nelson Santos, Dafna Steinberg, Joseph R. Wolin, and Joy Whalen.

Thank you to Samuel Anderson, Luke Mannarino, and Dana Stirling for helping me put it all together.

Special thanks to luke kurtis and bd-studios.com for making it possible for this book to exist in the world. We did it!

For any and all information
go to www.jonathandavidsmyth.com

Now That You've Gone and Come Back

Published by bd-studios.com in New York City, 2023
© Jonathan David Smyth

Photography, handwritten pieces + text by Jonathan David Smyth
Design + layout by luke kurtis
One-to-One series captured and digitized by Dana Stirling
Copy editor: Samuel Anderson
Photo editor + project assistant: Luke Mannarino

ISBN 978-1-950231-89-8

All Rights Reserved. No part of this publication may be reproduced,
stored in a retrieval system or transmitted in any form or by any
means without the prior permission in writing of copyright holders
and of the publisher.

www.ingramcontent.com/pod-product-compliance
Lightning Source LLC
Chambersburg PA
CBHW042049030726
47599CB00019B/2417